Build A Sculptured Low Back Chair

with charles brock

Furniture instructional bundle series. This book is a companion piece to the *Build A Sculptured Low Back Chair with Charles Brock* DVD, full-size patterns and online support.

dedication

This book and video are dedicated to Sheila, Emily, Steve, Keri and Ava. Thanks for your love and support!

special thanks to

Cecil Cheves
Chris Bagby
Mark McGowan
Stephen Price
Emily Brock
Peachstate Lumber
Festool USA
Kreg Tool Company
Whiteside Tool Company

contact

charlesbrockchairmaker.com

Visit to register for Chuck's studio membership, and to find out about updates and classes.

Tortoise & Chair Publications
A Division of Charles Brock, LLC
www.charlesbrockchairmaker.com

Editor, Cover & Interior Designer: Emily Brock
Associate Editor: Sheila Brock
Photographers: Mark McGowan, Kenny Gray, Charles Brock
Cover Photographer: Kenny Gray

Second Edition
2011, 2012

Build A Sculptured Low Back Dining Chair with Charles Brock
To be sold only as a Bundle of Companion Components:

Build A Sculptured Low Back Dining Chair with Charles Brock DVD
Build A Sculptured Low Back Dining Chair with Charles Brock Book
Build A Sculptured Low Back Dining Chair with Charles Brock Full-Size Patterns

Copyright © 2010, Charles Brock, LLC. All rights reserved.

Published by Tortoise and Chair Publications
6437 Fall Branch Drive, Columbus, GA 31904

ISBN: 978-0-578-06060-6

WARNING!

Woodworking can be very dangerous. It is your responsibility to take the proper precautions and to use appropriate judgment.

1. Never work in the shop while tired, sleepy or under the influence.
2. Use all guards that come with power tools when possible. Guards have been removed in the DVD and in the book for visual clarity.
3. Wood dust is a known carcinogen and can cause allergic reactions.
4. Appropriate shop glasses should be worn at all times.
5. Read the manuals that come with your tools and follow their directions.
6. Read the book and view the entire video before performing any of the tasks demonstrated or described.
7. Never perform a task seen in this video or described in the book that makes you feel uncomfortable.
8. Never wear loose clothing or jewelry while woodworking.

chapter one
Inspiration of the Sculptured Low Back Chair

figure 1.1

figure 1.2

Do you remember when you first saw a Sam Maloof Low Back Chair (Figure 1.1)? For me the experience was much different then my first encounter with the rocker. The Maloof rocker filled me with instant inspiration. The Low Back Chair was seen and remembered as "too contemporary for my taste". I was not inspired to place the project on my "bucket list" of fine woodworking projects. Sam always said he was most proud of this chair's design. If Sam said it was great it had to be special. My mind kept drifting to the lines and movement of this low back chair. For me, it was an acquired taste like a fine wine or asparagus if you will. When you grow to like it you love it! The low back chair has won my chair design heart.

The magic of the Low Back Chair is in its form and function like any classic design. The chair is at home in a set for the dining table or as an occasional chair. The lucky sitter is comfortable in the deeply sculpted seat and because of the backrest's wonderful lumbar support. The flowing lines of the backrest and arms sweep down and reach out making a wonderful invitation to the observer to sit and enjoy the occasion.

My taste for this design I must admit was primed by my desire to first build a rocker as inspired by Sam Maloof's work. A picture of one of my early rockers with Maloof inspired elements inspired a well-known woodworking school to call and offer me an opportunity to teach my rocker (Figure 1.2) to fine woodworkers. Since I was approaching retirement as an educator, this offer was exciting to me.

After teaching some classes, I published an instructional bundle based on the rocker Sam inspired me to build. My plan is to publish instructional bundles containing many of the pieces inspired by Sam's work. My goal is to assist woodworkers in building the furniture of their inspiration. The Low Back Dining Chair is a great member of this series and one of my most proud accomplishments as a woodworker and teacher (Figure 1.3).

figure 1.3

chapter two

Making Your Sculptured Low Back Dining Chair A Reality

As a teacher and woodworker my goal is to help you with your dream to build a sculptured low back dining chair (Figure 2.1). My purpose is to give you the knowledge and confidence to build your own chair by utilizing the four companion parts of the instructional bundle. Utilizing these instructional materials you should be able to:

1. Select and order wood for your chair project.
2. Cooper and sculpt a seat
3. Band saw and shape the front legs.
4. Band saw and duplicate the back legs.
5. Cut and assemble the signature seat to leg joinery.
6. Band saw, fit and shape the sweeping arms.
7. Bandsaw and shape the backrest.
8. Assemble chair with the proper glues, screws and plugs.
9. Fair all the chair parts together.

When you reach this point you should be able to shape and carve your chair with a final touch of your own artistry, knowledgeable of the chair's salient hard and soft lines, while utiizing the appropriate tools and methods.

figure 2.1

your bundle consists of

Full-Size Patterns
Book
Instructional DVD/Video
Online Support

All of these components work together facilitating your successful completion of the chair.

making the patterns

The patterns must be transferred to a thicker material to be used for tracing on to your stock. I use various materials depending on the way the particular pattern needs to be used. Use the list below to make your choice:

The back leg side profile should be made out of 1/4" to 3/4" hardwood plywood. This is especially important if you intend to trim your back leg with a copy bit at the router table. The extra thickness will give you plenty of bearing surface to support the pilot bearing.

The remainder of the patterns can be made from 1/8" hardwood plywood making them lightweight and flexible.

gluing the paper patterns to the material

Gluing the paper patterns to the plywood or other material can be tricky. A good spray adhesive made for paper will generally work well. Cut off a scrap from the pattern paper and test glue the paper to the plywood or pattern material. Test for open-time, adhesion, ability to make adjustments if necessary and general fitness for the task. Do not begin until you are satisfied with the results. After the paper patterns are mounted the inside surfaces must be sanded smooth to make tracing easy.

> **The following tools can make this process easier and are ordered by priority:**
>
> *An oscillating spindle sander for inside curves*
>
> *Sanding Block (100 grit paper)*
>
> *A stationary belt sander with an articulating table set to 90 degrees*
>
> *Rasps and files (both curved and flat surfaces)*
>
> *Microplanes (both curved and flat surfaces)*

the pattern making sequence

Rough cut the paper patterns leaving a 3/8" to 1/2" of an inch outside the line.

Glue the pattern to your choice of plywood or other material.

Band saw to the line before sanding the line smooth or until it just disappears.

Write any important measurements or other useful information such as rough stock sizing, right hand or left hand on the pattern. A date or style name can be very helpful in establishing benchmarks.

using the book

Although the video is worth a thousand words in this case, everything could not be included in the DVD. So I decided to write a book as its companion to further explain the process. The book includes details you will need: special measurements, hints, tool lists and my notes on each part of the process. I have also included a checklist for assembly and glue-up.

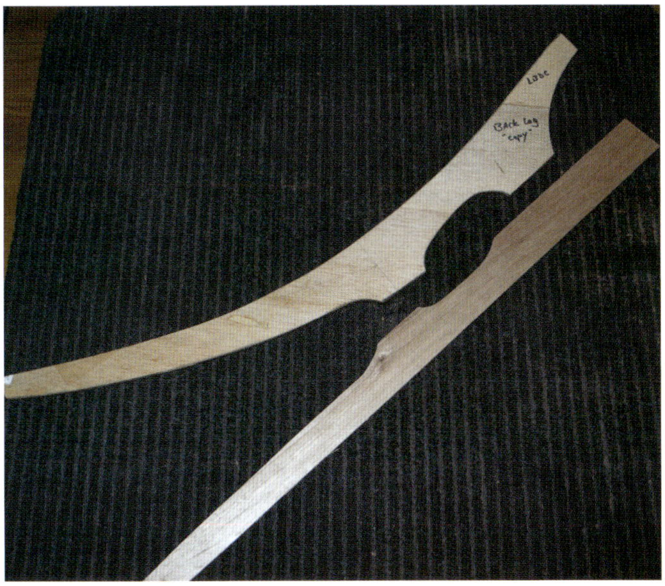

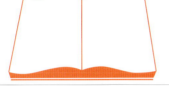
figure 2.2

Red Book Icon
figure 2.3

figure 2.4

using the DVD

The DVD is vital to the successful completion of the chair. Many woodworkers are strong visual learners because fine woodworking is a visual art. The best strategy would be to watch the entire video to get an overview of the project. Then watch "The Seat" and read the chapter. Treating each chair part, as a project and assembling them together following the assembly schedule should make the project a success. When you see the red book icon (Figure 2.3) on the video screen it means there is some very important information in the book that you must access. Look for the book icons in your book also.

the relationship between experience and success

I have tried not to suggest this project is suitable for a specific level of woodworker accomplishment. Anyone who practices a set of skills must push themselves towards a higher level of accomplishment. This is not a project for a beginner, and no woodworker I know classifies themselves as intermediate. You will know soon enough if this is within your ability to build. If the vocabulary and skills are new to you, study and complete other projects while you practice the skill sets. Soon you well be ready to begin your own chair.

selecting wood for your chair

Your choice of a primary wood is one of the most important decisions you will make short of the chair's actual design. Like everything it is about choices. Your choice should meet the standards of suitability for function and appearance. Some wood species just do not make good functional choices. Most softwoods and some hardwoods lack density and strength. Chair parts would have to be made more massive to withstand the rigors of stress. This is a chair of lines not mass so these woods do not meet the standards for function or appearance.

The signature wood used by Sam Maloof was walnut (figures 2.3). It exceeds the function as well as the appearance standards. It is strong and stable once it is properly dried and it works well with both hand and power tools. Walnut also takes a wonderful deep polish, as well as a beautiful oil and wax finish. There are many domestic walnut varieties to choose from such as Claro (a hybrid from California and Oregon,) English and black walnuts as well as some exotics. They can exhibit tremendous color ranges in their grain from black to all shades of brown to cream with juxtaposing shades of red, orange, yellow and even green. Dramatic figure can be found exhibiting swirling grain patterns, curl, crotches, feathers and combinations of all of these elements. Exotic walnuts are available in some U.S. locations, to provide more choices.

There are also drying choices such as air versus kiln.

Another consideration is steaming (evens out color with sapwood,) and using sapwood to your advantage. Air dried walnut is more of a red brown versus kiln dried which has a more purplish gray when fresh cut by shop tools. Other great choices are curly maple, figured cherry, white or brown oak, mesquite, rosewood and zircote.

The rocker requires 40 to 50 board feet of 8/4 stock. A cut sheet can be made from part specifications in each chapter. My recommendation is to purchase 8/4 stock in 6 – 10 inch widths. Most parts require 2 to 4 foot lengths.

With that in mind buy 6 to 10 foot lengths. It is a little harder to find, but 10/4 stock is best for the headrest (crest rail) and the arms. The extra half inch allows a deeper headrest radius and more of a sweep in the arms from joint to joint. You can laminate stock to accomplish this objective as shown in the video, but solid stock provides more continuity of grain and color.

I take my patterns to each board and look for the best matches for each part based on size, figure and grain orientation. I do not want short grain situations in the legs or any part that will be under stress from the sitter. My recommendation is to purchase 8/4 lumber in 6 – 10 inch widths. Most parts require 2 to 4 foot lengths. With that in mind buy 6 to 10 foot lengths. It is great if you are blessed with a source for 8/4 stock in the rough that mills down to a full 2 inches.

If your 8/4 lumber has been surfaced to 1 13/16" by a helpful dealer do not despair. You can build an outstanding chair with stock as thin as 1 ¾ of an inch.

Another way to purchase your stock is in the form of a slab. Usually slabs are cross-sections of the tree. They have live edges (see figure 2.5) sometimes with pieces of bark still clinging to them. You will usually find crotches where limbs grew out of the trunk, and swirling grain throughout the slab. I have used slabs as long as 17 feet long x 6 feet wide and 10/4 thick. The good news is you have great choices for laying out parts with your patterns that take advantage of the grain and figure.

The bad news unfortunately is cost. I have paid almost $80 per board foot for some outstanding air dried slabs. They work well with hand tools, and have great color. You will have more knots, splits and other problems to work around. Tinted epoxies and modern glues will cure most problems. I like to work with 10/4 thick slabs because it gives me enough room to work around problem areas. My recommendation is to use slabs after you become more experienced.

In addition to my primary stock, ebony makes a great looking plug to cover and enhance screw holes as part of the design. Now let's make a seat!

figure 2.4

chapter three

Assembling and Coopering the Seat

figure 3.1

The seat, or more romantically "the saddle," is where you begin to craft your chair. It invites the sitter with its exciting contours and is the proud recipient of the visible joinery that flows into the front and back legs (Figure 3.1). If you have built the sculptured rocker, the coopered seat is the same with the exception of the lack of spindle mortises.

The first question here is whether you want to cooper the seat with five boards or make a flat panel seat. The coopered seat (see Figure 3.2) provides a more concave appearance which is even more inviting to the sitter. It also lowers the pommel by almost 3/8", which allows it to stand proud without getting in the way of the sitter. The flat panel seat (see figure 3.1) is much easier. My first few chairs had flat panel seats and were well received.

Most observers will not even know about the coopered seat option. Build the flat panel the same as the coopered seat, but do not bevel any board edges. The finished seat panel should be 20" wide x 22" long and ideally 2" thick no matter which type of seat construction you choose. If you choose to make a wider seat than 20 inches, the major change will be in the width of the headrest and the possibly the spacing of the spindle mortises on the headrest.

Using the seat pattern is simple. Find the center of the seat blank and mark a center line. Line up and draw the center using the pattern and the outside boundaries of the bowl by marking one side and flipping it over to mark the other side of the blank.

steps in assembling and preparing a seat blank

1 Mill five boards 4 1/4" x 22" x 2" and organize for appearance. Placing seat boards with different grain together (juxtapositional diversity) can be as wonderful as the flow of similar grain patterns and color. Your boards must be four square before you continue!

2 Label the seat boards 1 through 5. Use chalk or white art pencils so the marking will pop-out. Also, mark the boards to be beveled. I exaggerate the bevel when marking them to make sure I place the bevels where I want them.

3 Decide whether to cut the bevels on a table saw or on a jointer. Set the table saw blade or jointer fence (Figure 3.2) to three degrees using a sliding bevel and a Bevel Boss or it's equivalent (Figure 3.3).

4 Cut three degrees off of each edge of board 3 as shown in the video. If you use the jointer, make marks across the edge of the board and stop jointing when you have removed all the marks using light cuts. I like the jointer because I would still need to joint the surfaces after I cut them on the table saw.

5 Bevel the outside edges of boards 2 and 4.

6 Put a clamp on them to make sure the joints are tight and you have produced the required concave appearance or "Smile." Boards 1 and 5 should be in the same flat plane.

7 Find the center of the coopered seat panel and rip and joint an equal amount of material from boards 1 and 5 to arrive at the 20" seat width.

8 Make reference or witness marks that can be used to align the boards throughout the project. A centerline from the pommel to the back of the seat and a line across the width of the seat about two inches from the back of the seat. This line should line up in the heat of gluing-up without fail.

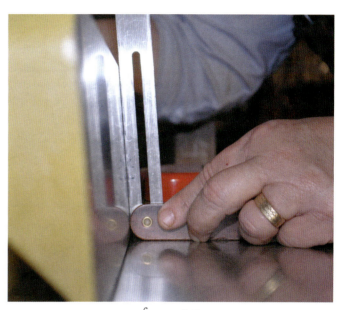

figure 3.2

figure 3.3

9 You have choices to make for reinforcement. If you have a horizontal boring machine or a ShopSmith you've got it made. A Festool Domino (as shown in the video) works great, but is expensive. Biscuit joiners are used much the same way as the Domino but more biscuits are necessary for strength. Freud makes a Dowel Jointer that works in much the same way as a biscuit or Domino.

10 Place 3 Dominoes (# 8x40 mm) in each joint ½" from the boards bottom starting 5" from the back of the seat and spacing them 6" apart. Five biscuits (#20) or 3 dowels (3/8 or ½") will do the job nicely, too. If you are using the domino, dowel jointer or biscuits practice on some scraps with bevels. Boards 2 and 4 require you to flip them over and set the fence to their obtuse angle (Figure 3.4). Adjust the depth from the fence until you place the domino (10mm) or biscuit to match up precisely with the mortises or slots on boards 1 and 5. Your choice of reinforcement will also make it possible to glue-up the panel, especially if it is coopered. Gluing up the beveled panels without reinforcement will result in problems. After dry fitting, you are ready to start cutting the joinery.

Note: Do not glue up yet as you will ruin your opportunity to cut the seat joinery!

11 Lay out the back (2 1/2" wide x 3" long x 2" thick) (Figure 3.5) and front (1/4" X 1 3/4" long x 2" thick) (Figure 3.6) notches on boards 1 and 5. The front notch starts 18 inches from the back of the seat board. Mark all lines with a marking knife or gauge. Highlight the cut lines in white (on walnut) for better visibility.

figure 3.4

figure 3.5

figure 3.6

Using a cross-cut sled, or miter gauge with a tall fence, cut the back notch by first clamping the board on end and making a rip cut 2 7/8" along the cut line (Figure 3.7). I leave this cut short of 3" so the cross-cut at 2 1/2" will take the piece out. I kerf out the front notches using a crosscut sled on the table saw as shown in the video.

12 Trim the kerf lines from the front leg notches with a router plane, shoulder plane or chisel.

13 The notches must be rabbeted with a 1/2" radius router bit. Rabbeting the top and bottom of each notch at the same depth with a plunge router will leave a tenon (Figure 3.8) at each notch location. I shoot for 1 inch and mark them out as shown in the video. You may choose a different size tenon. The rabbeting bit and round-over bit used must have matching diameters. The tool list in the appendix contains a rabbet and round-over bit combination that matches.

Note: Be careful of tear-out! As the rabbet bit finishes the cut, short grain situations can cause chip out. Most chip out will occur in areas that will be rounded over but a sacrificial block clamped on to the area can prevent this from happening. You may also add on a quarter of an inch and rip it off before glue-up. I usually pull out short of the end of the cut (as shown in the video) when rabbeting the back notches because these areas are waste. You may have trouble balancing the router during the rabbeting of the rear notches. Clamp another seat board to the board you are routing to give your router more bearing surface.

figure 3.7

figure 3.8

figure 3.9

15 Lay your pattern on top of the seat blank and draw the centerline first followed by the boundary lines for sculpting your seat's bowl. Mark a centerline on the back and bottom of the seat blank now for reference later.

No glue yet because now you are going to save yourself a lot of dust and work by sawing out seat waste with your band saw (as shown in the video).

16 Start with board 3 by making all four band saw cuts (Figure 3.9). Then lay 2 and 4 next to 3 in left to right sequence. The trick is to swap 2 with 4 to trace along their edge using the edge of board 3 as a template. This will give you a flat cut on boards 2 and 4 instead of cutting with the 3-degree bevel down. Do not start your band saw cut at the back of the bowl line on 2 and 4. Start your cut even with the most forward marked edge of the back of the seat bowl. Then use 2 and 4 to trace the inside edge of 1 and 5.

Ideally you should have an inch of thickness in the deepest part of the bowl. About 2/3 of the way to the front, it should be approximately 1 1/4" thick with a quick taper toward the front of the seat.

17 Use a grinder to remove excess seat material around the pommel on #3, the back of the seat bowl line on 2 & 4 (Figure 3.10) and the material on the inside edge of boards 1 & 5. Don't be a hero and remove too much. When its glued up you will have a chance to smooth and even everything out.

18 Glue-up the seat panel. Titebond III works well. Use plenty of clamps and check that all witness marks line-up. The rule is to plan well and work quickly! The clamping jig (Figure 3.11) is very helpful because it allows clamping the centerboard down and applying pressure to the outside of 1 and 5 without lifting their edges.

figure 3.11

carving a seat

This part of the project is exciting, interesting, rigorous, and can be bad for your health! Please use dust collection and wear an appropriate air filtration device. Please do not have any loose hanging clothing that the grinder can snatch. I have a t-shirt that shows what it can do!

1 Use a grinder with 24 grit paper or a donut shaped, coarse carbide grinding wheel. Start removing stock from the boundary lines first on boards 1 and 5 by working from the line toward the middle with a rolling motion. Make a simple depth gauge for checking depth and symmetry (see Appendix for specs). Cross grain strokes are better for rough shaping while light strokes with the grain can smooth surfaces.

2 Finish carving the seat bowl, front and underside to taste using tools such as the ones in (figure 3.12). Sand all finished areas of the seat to 400 grit.

figure 3.10

GOUGES	POWER CARVING BURRS	FLAP SANDING WHEELS	SCRAPERS
Gouges are great for cross grain work such as defining the concave area of the seat, and the edge of the seat's bowl.	Burrs, especially the larger coarse and extra coarse carbide bullnose profiles can be used to advantage to efficiently shape concave areas of the seat.	(80 & 120 grit) These aid the process of shaping the seat's curves but with more control. The Guinevere round inflatable sander with a 60 grit-sanding sleeve mounted in a flex-shaft die grinder is my favorite for smoothing the seat radii.	In particular, gooseneck, convex and concave scrapers smooth the high spots. Used correctly scrapers cut instead of abrade leaving an almost finished surface.

figure 3.12

chapter four

Crafting A Set of Chair Legs

front legs

The Low Back Chair's front legs (figure 4.1) are not the traditional Maloof front legs because of their sweep toward the front of the chair. Sam's chair was usually shown with a tapered turned leg. The seat to leg joinery is dimensionally different but the elements are the same.

Your choice is deciding which leg you would like to make. The turned leg is like the one on the rocker except for the length above and below the joint. Use the pattern in the bundle. Follow all the instructions except for the following:

Don't trace the sweep taper below the joint. Instead, Draw two parallel lines extending from below the seat to leg joint to the bottom of the leg. These lines will be 7/8" from the centerline. Band saw on these lines to make a new side profile pattern.

Do not use the front profile. Instead, remove 1/4" from the inside bottom of the leg below the leg joint and above the leg joint. Find the centers on each end and draw 1 1/4" circles. Turn the tapers on a lathe using the centers and staying clear of the joint area.

One reason I chose to design the front leg with a sweep is that so many fine woodworkers wanted to build a sculptured rocker who didn't have a lathe. This leg's construction doesn't require one and I believe the legs sweep adds to the movement of the chair in a positive way. The highback dining chair will have the same leg, making for a complimentary set.

figure 4.1

steps for crafting a sweeping front leg

1 Mill Appropriate Stock to 2@ 2"X 2 13/16"X 21" 90-Degrees on each end. Draw the pattern on the potential stock to check the grain orientation. Orient any grain movement in the direction of the sweep at the bottom of the leg. Don't settle for any short grain in the lower leg's sweep.

2 I always leave an extra 1/16" in width when I mill up the front leg stock so it will have to be jointed to just slide between the shoulders of the seat rabbets.

3 Prominently label your legs right (R) and left (L) inside (I) and outside (O). The orientation is based on a person sitting in the chair. Their right hand would be on the right armrest.

4 Use a wheel type marking gauge to mark a centerline on the inside, outside and ends of both pieces of leg stock.

5 On the inside of one leg, layout the top line of the dado. Measure 3 " from the top and make a tick mark with a marking knife. Cut a line and carry it to all four sides.

6 Transfer this line with a square to the inside of the other leg and cut lines all the way around.

7 Measure the tenon on the seat joint with dial calipers (figure 4.2). Don't clamp the caliper's jaws tightly around the tenon. Make it a little loose because you will be using the inside points of the caliper's jaws to set the point for the bottom of the dado. Just make a tick mark and use this point to cut lines all the way around the leg. Be sure to measure the other seat tenon the same way incase there are differences.

8 Mark the depth of the dados at 1/2" on 3 sides. Outline them with a white pencil to make the cut line stand out. Do not outline the outside of the leg's dado all the way across. The outside of the leg will have depth lines and Xs (Figure 4.3).

9 You will need a cross cut sled that cuts at 90-degrees to cut the dados. Check that your blade is cutting at 90 degrees from the sled top, too. Set the cut height by making a cut between the cut-lines and raising the blade a little each time until it just nicks the bottom of the depth line. Kerf out the stock between the cut lines on the inside and two adjacent sides of the leg (Figure 4.4).

> **BEST PRACTICES**
> *Before you make any cut ask yourself, "What I am I trying to accomplish with this cut? Will this cut achieve the goal? If you are not sure, stop!*

figure 4.2

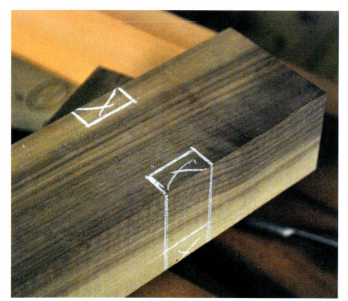

figure 4.3

figure 4.4

figure 4.5

10 Test the dado to see if it will slip over the tenon. It not take off more toward the bottom of the leg. This is where a zero clearance cross cut sled comes in handy.

11 When it slips on snug but not too tight the bottoms of the dados must be cleaned. Use a router plane (Figure 4.5). To set the depth, place a playing card on each dado shoulder and loosen the knurled knob on the plane letting the cutter bottom out in the dado . Tighten the knob, remove the cards and clean up the kerfs. Try to work with the grain.

12 Round over the inside of each joint with a 3/4" router bit at the router table. Make sure you get the full round-over by neutralizing the bit's pilot bearing and setting the bit height to the tabletop as shown in the DVD.

13 On the outside face of the leg mark one or two points with an awl on the centerline 3/32" inside each of the dado cut lines scored across the front of the leg. At the drill press using a Miller 1X (or 1XJ) drill bit, drill through the leg and stop at the collar on the drill bit.

14 You will finish profiling the leg later.

back legs

The chair's back legs (figure 4.1) really set all the movement in motion. They provide joint locations for all parts except for the front legs. The lower leg provides a wonderful sweep while the upper leg lifts up and clears out for the arm return and sweep of the backrest. The 90-degree seat to leg joint is traditional for this chair, although the tapered profile on the inside of the bottom of the leg is not. The objective for adding the taper was to compliment a similar taper on the inside of the front leg.

steps for crafting the back leg

1 Prepare stock (minimum) 2 @ 2"x 6 1/2" X 30 1/8"

Note: Stock doesn't have to be squared on the ends. The most important factors are grain orientation in the lower leg and enough stock.

2 Trace the outline of the back leg onto the stock and band saw leaving 1/16 to 1/32" of the line.

figure 4.6

METHOD 1	METHOD 2	METHOD 3	MAKE A SEQUENCING DECISION & EITHER
Duplicate the leg at the router table with a spiral copy bit. Make your pattern out of some 1/4" (or thicker) plywood. Add about 1 1/2" to the length of the pattern and stock at each end of the leg and attach the pattern to the leg with screw and or double stick turner's tape. Route just past the end of each leg. Kickback can be a problem at the top and bottom of the leg with a 2" bit at the router table.	Attach the pattern with double stick tape (Figure 4.6) and remove the line with a large coarse rasp. (As shown on the video) Use a hand plane to true the arm and seat joint stems to the pattern. They must be 90-degrees to the sides of the leg and perfectly flat. If not the leg will wobble while cutting the dados on the table saw.	You might use the router table to true the arm and seat joint stems using a 1/2" thick or better pattern and band saw and rasp the rest.	Trace and bandsaw the front back leg profile (Go to Step 11 and Return to Step 5) OR Layout and cut the back leg dados on the table saw. (Go to Step 5)

figure 4.7

figure 4.8

figure 4.9

📖 It is much easier to cut the dados in the back leg before you bandsaw the front profile for the back leg. You can cut the dados as in the DVD first or flip-flop these steps. The decision has to do with balance while you kerf out the dados. This sequence will allow the back leg to sit flush against the fence for the front of the seat to leg dado and against the bed of the crosscut sled when you cut the inside seat to leg dados. Either way, use the outboard leg support with a clamp to support the end of the leg.

5 Start the blackleg to seat joint layout. First find the center of the top of the back leg. Make a pencil mark. Then measure 14 3/8" to the outside of the outside front edge of the seat joint stem and make a pencil mark. This is the top of your dado on the back leg. Mark it with a cutline using a square. Extend the cutline to the front of the back leg seat joint stem.

6 Orient the other back leg so that it lines up with the one you have marked and transfer the cut line to the other leg. Remember you are making a pair of legs.

7 Measure the appropriate seat tenon with the dial calipers (not too tight) and use cut lines to layout the width of the dados out on the inside of the back leg stem as shown in the video. Don't forget to make cut lines to show the depth of the dados because that's where you will be lining up your cut at the table saw. Measure each seat tenon to layout the width of each dado. Use an appropriate color pencil to highlight the cut lines so you can see them.

8 Set your table saw blade to make a 1/2"

figure 4.10

figure 4.11

deep cut by raising it up a little at a time until you just break the bottom of the depth cut line. Remove the material on the front of the leg first. Use the outboard support block to steady the end of the leg (Figure 4.7). Then attach a piece of scrap or the long edge of the outboard support (Figure 4.8) to the outside of the leg to steady it while you cut the dado on the inside of the leg (Figure 4.9).

9 Test the dado to see if it fits the tenon. If it doesn't, take off very thin cuts toward the bottom of the leg until it does.

10 Clean up the dado bottoms with a router plane. Note: Place a playing card on each dado shoulder and loosen the knurled knob on the pane letting the cutter bottom out in the dado. Tighten the knob, remove the cards and clean up the kerfs. Try to work with the grain.

11 Layout and band saw the front back leg profiles and use a rasp to fair them smooth as shown in the video.

12 Round-over the inside of the back leg joint stems at the router table as shown in the video. Be sure to again use a piece of plywood scrap or the long edge of the outboard support block attached to the leg with double stick turner's tape.

13 At the drill press, pre-drill two holes in the outside of the back leg at the seat joint with the Miller Bit down to the collar . To layout the locations for these holes, first find the center of the dado location and draw a line perpendicular to the bottom of the dado toward the back of the leg. The hole locations are at 3/4" and 1 3/4" along that line. Mark them with an awl.

steps for fitting the front and back legs

1 There are generally two surface areas that keep the legs from fitting. The depth of the dados (sometimes) and the rounded over shoulders on the insides of the legs (almost always) need fitting.

2 Try a test fit. If the joint is too tight, observe the
joint surfaces for shiny spots that will denote tight areas.

3 For depth problems use the router plane to cutter a little deeper. For problems with the round over use a sanding block and 100 - 150 grit paper to round those shoulders until they fit snug against the seat rabbet shoulders.

steps for legging up

NO GLUE YET!
1 Place the seat on a solid surface using hand screws to steady the seat in a vertical position. Place each leg in the appropriate place and finish predrilling into the seat. The upper front leg hole should not be drilled to full depth in the seat. Attach each leg with #10x3" Spax screws with the exception of the upper front leg hole which receives a #10x 2 1/2" screw.

2 Turn the chair over on the other side and repeat the same sequence.

3 Trace a red line at the top and bottom of each leg to seat joint. (Figure 4.10)

Yes, you can sit down on it carefully. You are legged up! (Figure 4.11)

chapter five
Profiling the Front Leg

figure 5.1

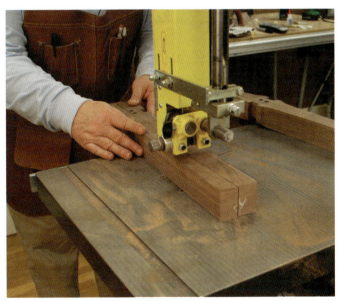

figure 5.2

steps for profiling the front leg

The profiling of the front leg will prepare the leg for shaping and attachment to the arm with a dowel.

1 Label one side of the front leg's side profile right (R) and the other side left (L) based on the sweep at the bottom of the leg. The right side sweeps to your right and the left sweeps to your left.

2 Lay the pattern over the outside of the leg and trace the outline.

3 Using the centerline that you scored around the leg earlier, find the center of the top of the leg and mark it with an awl. Also scribe a line 1/4" in from the outside and inside of the top of the leg. Highlight all of these lines and points with a colored pencil for clarity. Use a compass and draw a 5/8" radius circle from the center point just to get an idea of the finished size of the top of the leg.

4 Using a Dowel-It (Figure 5.1) or a drill press, drill a 1/2"X 1 1/4" hole in the top of the leg using a brad point drill bit.

5 Band saw the outside profile on the line (Figure 5.2). Although it is not necessary you may want to use a rasp to clean up the saw marks.

6 Trace the front, front leg profile (Figure 5.3). The taper flows to the bottom of the leg starting with the inside of the leg at the seat to leg joint about 5/8" below the dado. It gives the look of a slight splay.

7 Make this cut at the band saw careful to use the seat to leg joint as a means of supporting a square cut in this area (as shown in the video).

8 Using your finger as a fence, trace the 1/4" that was marked across the top inside of the leg down each side of the leg curving out 5/8" above the seat to joint area. This will supply the offset on the inside of the front leg that will be sculpted to curve up and provide the pedestal for the arm. It also will provide a location for lining up the inside of the sweeping curve of the arm.

figure 5.3

chapter six

Shaping and Fitting the Arms

figure 6.1

BEST PRACTICES
Remember to ask if making the cut you are about to make will create an arm the appropriate right or left hand arm.

The most riveting element of this chair's design is the compound curve of the chair's arms. They at once make the chair contemporary, sweeping down in an arc and back up lifting the observer's eyes in the process. They are easily the most difficult test for the craftsman of this chair. Not only is the arm's radius a compound curve, it is joined to the back leg at a compound angle.

I have tried to simplify the fitting process, but it still requires a pragmatic effort. Watch the video chapter and read the chapter in its entirety to help form your strategy.

My only regret is that there is too much wasted wood. Knowing woodworkers the way I do, I can see a lot of pens, pepper mills and such turned out of the off-cuts.

steps for shaping and fitting the arm

1 Mill your stock: 2@ 8/4 X 6 3/4" X 22" Square both ends as a "Best Practice."

Note: It is longer than necessary for a purpose. While fitting the compound angle joint, the extra stock could come into play to give you some wiggle room.

2 Pick some stock with grain that moves in a sweeping curve complimentary to the pattern if possible. Trace the pattern on the potential arm stock and examine the grain.

3 Clamp the board to the top of the front leg (Figure 6.1). Let the back of the board run past the inside of the back leg's arm stem. Hold something flat against the face of the arm stem and scribe a line on the arm. The purpose is to identify the arm angle. The angle will probably be about 7 1/2 degrees. The angle could vary because of a number of variables. That is why it's important to be able to identify the actual angle as opposed to what it is supposed to be.

4 Use a sliding bevel to copy the angle and for setting your table saw's miter gauge. Make the first cut at the back of the board not on the angled line you traced (Figure 6.2). Now check to see if the outside edge of the miter lines up tight against the outside of the arm stem on the back leg (Figure 6.3). Clamp the board to the top of the front leg again to check. Mark the outside of the arm board and also mark the arm right or left. Don't cut the angle on the other arm board at this time.

Fit one arm completely before moving to the other. If the miter fits go on to step 5. If not, examine the front face of the arm stem. Is it flat in all directions? Is it 90 degrees to the side of the back leg? If not use a block plane to make it flat and square.

Fit one arm completely before moving to the other. If the miter fits go on to step 5. If not, examine the front face of the arm stem. Is it flat in all directions? Is it 90 degrees to the side of the back leg? If not use a block plane to make it flat and square.

Then, identify the angle and set the miter gauge and try again. Cut off a little at a time until it fits.

5 Leave your miter gauge set from the first cut. First try Method A for finishing the compound arm cut. If the arm doesn't cross the front leg try Method B. You may want to perfect your strategy and identify your angles with a piece of 2" x 8" framing stock.

figure 6.2

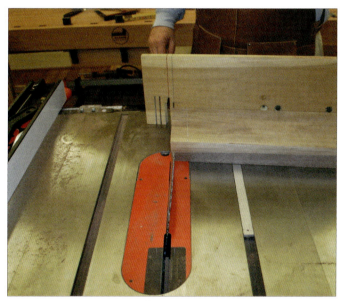
figure 6.3

Method A

Next, tilt your table saw blade to make an 8-degree cut. The table saw used on the video tilts to the left (Figure 6. 4). Rethink the miter gauge and tilt set up if your saw tilts to the right side. The objective is to cut the second angle (tilt) as you recut the first angle (miter gauge) simultaneously. Your cut should form an obtuse angle from the face of the outside of the arm stock. In the picture I marked the red line running to the outside of the board shows the direction of the second cut's angle (Figure 6. 5) to help me with orienting the cut at the table saw. The angle should swing the arm out toward the top of the front leg if successful.

Method B

As shown in the video: Use the sliding bevel to identify the open angle for the second cut. Place the side of the sliding bevel on the outside of the back leg. With the outside edge of the back of the arm stock clamped into the place against the outside edge of the arm stem, place the bevel's blade against the back of the arm board and lock it into place. Use the bevel to set the tilt of your table saw blade. Cut this angle so as to form an obtuse angle (greater than 90 degrees) with the outside face of the arm board.

figure 6.4

6 Complete the fitting of both arms.

7 Use the top arm profile to layout the inside radius to be cut at the band saw (as shown in the video). Make sure your saw allows a minimum of 6 1/2" under its guides. A 1/2" blade for this may be required for this heavy cut. Make the cut taking it slow and feeding the radius along the line.

figure 6.5

8 Glue the off-cut from the inside of the arm to the outside of the arm board as shown in the video. The bottom edges must be clamped flat so as not to effect the front and back leg fit. Use plenty of clamps. Let it sit for 24 hours.

9 Clamp the arm in place. The back of the arm should fit flush against the back leg stem and the radius should curve around and cross the top of the front leg. Make sure the arm crosses the front leg top either flush with the 1/4" that has been removed on the inside of the leg or falls or no more than 1/4" to the outside of the line as in the picture (Figure 6. 6). If it doesn't don't fret. You can re-cut the compound angle to make it fit because you have flats on the inside at each end of the curved arm board you just glued up. Note: If the arm will not fit on your table saw top on the left side of the blade use a 3/4" piece of plywood as a base to lay the arm on (inside down) to make the cut.

figure 6.6

10 When the curved arm board fits, place a 1/2" dowel center in the top of the front leg (Figure 6.7) and set the arm in place. Tap the top of the board firmly to locate the arm to front leg dowel location. Use a Dowel-It or a drill press to drill a 1/2" X 1 1/4" hole at 90 degrees in the bottom of the arm. Note: In this case do not clamp the Dowel-It on the board. Just use it to steady the drill at 90 degrees for drilling.

figure 6.7

11 Layout and band saw the side arm profile as shown on the video (Figure 6.8). Make sure the stock is well supported during the cut.

figure 6.8

chapter seven
Crafting the Backrest

The arms and the back legs attach to the backrest and it becomes a focal point for the movement and invitation that this chair makes to an observer (Figure 7.1). The backrest is also a major contributor to the comfort and interest that makes it a contemporary masterpiece. The bottom profile provides great lumbar support as well as symmetrical beauty because of its dramatic sweeping downward curve. This echoes the arm's sweep that gives the chair an organic look that reminds me of a tulip (figure 7.2).

figure 7.1

steps in crafting the backrest

1 Mill stock to 8/4 X 7 1/8" X 14 1/2" Square the ends of the stock.

Note: This is a place to show off a beautiful piece of wood. Look for a piece that has an interesting plunging grain pattern.

2 There is no splay in the back legs. This makes it possible to attach the backrest to the back legs with 90- degree butt joints and screws. The first thing to do is make sure your back legs are at 90- degrees to the seat. If not you will have to find the angles as shown in the video. Slight differences can be remedied with clamping pressure. If they are square to the seat, go to step 3.

Note: Variations in the seat to back leg angle is usually a product of seat boards 1 and 5 being lifted up when clamping the seat together.

3 Measure the distance between the legs and cut the backrest stock to fit using the crosscut sled. When it fits, find the center of the stock and mark it out all the way around the backrest. Layout the front and back radii pattern on the top of the backrest and cut them at the band saw. You will need a minimum of 7 1/8" under your guides to accomplish this cut. Mark your centerline again.

4 Layout the top and bottom profiles with the seat pattern and cut them at the band saw.

figure 7.2

chapter eight
Profiling the Seat and Assembling the Chair

This is where a lot of details are taken care of so the chair can be assembled. Be sure to see the appendix to review the Glue-up Schedule.

figure 8.1

1 First, let's finish preparing the seat by legging up again and making some marks with a colored pencil on the inside and out side of all the seat to leg joints. The back of the seat needs a radius, the sides need to be trimmed to a nice profile, the thigh relief cutouts need to be cutout and a lot of rounding over needs to be done. Make your marks on the seat and the legs. These marks will identify where to cut and where not to cut.

2 After marking, take the chair apart and begin profiling the seat by using the back of the backrest radius pattern to draw a radius for the back of the seat. Use the centerline and connect the marks on the seat that identify the back of the back legs.

3 Band saw the radius staying about 1/16" outside the line at the seat joints. You may need to sand the back of the seat at the centerline because the saw has a tendency to cut through at this point.

4 Trace a profile down each side of the seat between the front and back legs using the pattern or make your own. It is an s-curve that starts at the back leg joint. Band saw the profile staying 1/16" outside the pattern line at the seat to leg joints.

5 Using the pattern trace and band saw the thigh relief cutouts on the seat front.

figure 8.2

6 Scrape the glue off the bottom of the seat and sand the seat boards to a smooth radius so you will have a good surface for rounding over the back of the seat with a handheld router. Use a 3/4" to 1" radius rounding over bit to knock off the edge at the back of the seat and down the side. Start and stop about an inch clear of the seat to leg joints. The purpose is to get a head start on removing material. These are not finished surfaces yet.

7 Prepare two dowels (Figure 8.1) for the front leg to arm joints. I use 1/2" oak dowels from the hardware store. They need to be cut to length (2 1/4"), sized, (to a true 1/2") fluted and chamfered on their ends. I use a special plate that sizes, flutes and chamfers (as shown in the video). After the video was made I took the legs off of it. They just get in the way. These steps are important because dowels are rarely accurately sized, and there must be places for the glue to go when the joint is closed. Vertical flutes move more glue faster than spiral flutes so I prefer to make my own dowels. The hydraulic pressure caused by the compression of two surfaces covered in glue can cause blowout.

8 Insert the dowels into the front leg to arm joints. No glue yet! Clamp the leg to arm joint with a light duty clamp. Place a large hand screw in the middle of the arm. Clamp the lower jaw to the seat (Figure 8.2). Don't over tighten. The arm to back leg joint should pull up flush. To identify the location of the back leg to arm screw hole, use a flexible measuring device like a folding rule and flex it against the back leg starting at the bottom. The location should be marked with an awl at 24" from the bottom and 1 " from the

figure 8.3

outside of the leg. Wrap blue tape around a 7/16" brad point drill bit exposing 1 1/4" of the bit. Drill a hole straight into the blackleg toward the center of the stabilized arm up to the tape and stop. Next use the Miller Dowel 1X (or 1XJ) drill bit to finish off the hole into the arm. Insert a #10 X3" Spax screw and tighten it up slowly.

9. Using the back leg pattern, identify and mark the backrest screw holes on the back legs (Figure 8.3). Place the backrest between the back legs and push it up toward the top of the legs. Loosely clamp the backrest at the same angle as the screw holes.

10. Place a 3/4" piece of plywood across the width of the seat and pull it up even with the front of the back leg notch. Use the top of this board as a reference point for identifying the backrest's ideal location. Set a sliding bevel to 110- degrees. Placing one of its legs on the board. Place the other against the face of the backrest. The front edges of the backrest should sit slightly in front of the back legs at the top and the bottom of the backrest should sit about 6 " above the centerline marked at the back of the seat's surface. Tighten the clamp and sit on the seat. Keeping in mind the bottom edge of the backrest is square; judge the backrest placement for comfort. Tweak its placement until you are satisfied. Pre-drill the screw holes with the Miller Dowel Bit. Sight down the curve in the backrest as you drill toward the center of the backrest. Drive the #10x3" Spax screws. No glue yet!

chapter nine
Sculpting the Chair

Except for the first two chapters, each chapter has sequentially followed the video adding explanation to each step of the construction process. This chapter is different because the video is designed to show the process of sculpting the chair utilizing a three-step approach (Figure 9.1).

1 Describe each view of a finished chair.

2 Planning the sculpting of each view on a rough chair form.

3 Sculpting of each chair view with many different hand and power carving tools.

4 Complete the three workbook activities in the book's appendix.

The purpose of the first half of this chapter is to share concepts designed to help you improve your ability to recognize the chair you desire to sculpt (Figure 9.2) and to make it a reality!

figure 9.1

lines shadows and curves

A graduate of one of the most prestigious woodworking schools in the U.S. recently wrote me to ask for help. I am not sure how he arrived at having constructed a roughed out Maloof type chair since he was inquiring about my instructional bundle. He was fearful of shaping and sculpting the legs, seat, etc. and then fairing one into the other. You know the tried and true FDR saying, "The only thing you have to fear is fear itself!" Sometimes we are afraid of failure and sometimes we are actually afraid of success. It is the old writers block, only in this case sculptor's block.

figure 9.2

Let me qualify this as a discussion of art over engineering. The engineering qualities of the woodworker are very necessary and should have gotten you and your chair to this point. This is more about freeing oneself from formula to producing what looks good to you and hopefully other observers.

Does nature or nurture make a wood sculptor? A man sat in the back of one of my Sculptured Rocker Demo Classes for a day and a half before raising his hand and stating, "I can put it together but I can't shape it!" He went on to describe his totally frustrated attempts to do anything art related.

What are the human tools necessary for success as a sculptor of wood? Sight is huge but not totally necessary. If you can see the line or visualize it, you are ready to pick up the tools and sculpt. This is the old idea stating that the sculptor removes everything that is not the chair. If this doesn't work for you, you must become a student of sight. Try this activity.

Most cars are automotive sculpture. Follow the hard lines (Figure 9.2) they define the hard lines (edges or movement) and how they pull the eye around the car. Find the softer (soft) lines and how they cause transitions to be made from surface to surface or hard line to hard line.

> **ANSWER THESE QUESTIONS ABOUT EACH CAR'S LINES & SURFACES:**
>
> 1 How are the lines the same?
>
> 2 How are they different?
>
> 3 Observe how opposing surfaces meet. Does the line caused by the meeting of two surfaces have different radii?
>
> 4 What surfaces are concave?
>
> 5 Which are convex?
>
> 6 Where are the flat surfaces?
>
> 7 Where are the shadows?
>
> 8 What causes the shadows?

Make visual comparisons of two cars that are in a competing group. Observe a Camry and a Honda. This will really work well if both cars are the same color.

Train your powers of observation. Now describe the lines and decide their purposes in the over-all design. Do the same thing with nature. Trees, leaves, flowers all have shapes, lines and surfaces in opposition. How do they work together to form the whole?

Touch is a huge human tool and can be your number one choice if you have a vision deficit! When I started studying Sam Maloof's work I saw them in a museum setting and I explored Sam's chairs kinesthetically. I touched and rubbed them with my fingers every time the security guard turned his head. I was using my fingers to get the details.

Touching it is a method for programming the lines into memory. As I sculpt I am always touching and asking myself how does it feel? Is it flat, hollow, round? How does this surface transitionto the next?

Get a ball of modeler's clay and form surfaces in opposition that you like and form a line at the transition between the two. Visualize, think and feel, and you are on your way!

start with the hard lines and a rasp

I see chair sculpting in four phases:

1 Construction
2 Hard Lines
3 Soft Lines
4 Transitions

During the construction phase you make the chair's parts and join them using the band saw, table saw, lathe and other tools. Many of the hard lines are formed by this construction phase (Figure 9.3), which ends with parts joined to each other.

But most of these hard lines need to be transformed or sculpted so they form a flow from one part to the other. At this point you should have the chair legged up with all of the rough shaping and profiling complete. No parts should be glued to the chair's seat. The arms and backrest should be attached with screws and the arm to front leg joint should be held with an unglued dowel.

Where do you begin? Pick up a tool and see what happens.

We are back to the fear problem unless we just jump in and take a chance. Is everybody going to be good at it? No! There isn't a lot to risk in comparison to many things we endeavor to do, but a lot to gain by trying.

Start with the side view as shown on the video. Pick one of these two areas to work first:

1 Start with the arm by rounding it over on top. Draw the lines as shown in the video and place the arm in a vice leg joint end up. Start with long strokes with a large rasp or angle grinder with either a carbide wheel or 24 - 36 grit sandpaper.

2 The front leg to seat joint requires greater control. Decide whether to remove the excess dado material on the sides of the front legs on the chair or off. I can remove more material more quickly off the chair but I know where I am going with each move. It is easier to visualize on the chair but a little harder to remove.

I use white and red pencils and black permanent markers on walnut to show these contours and to guide my work. Use pictures of the chair's views to help you draw useful lines as I did in the video. You can even decide that each color has meaning. Black means a hard or soft line. White is for contour and red means don't remove anymore from this area.

Every view has the same thought processes. Should I remove the part for shaping and then assemble it for fairing? What do I want to remove? What is my goal when it is gone?

figure 9.3

Are there lines that will flow from this part into the next? What tools can I use? Which tool is the quickest? How much control do I need to sculpt this area? Which tool will give me the most control?

When I am unsure of finding my chair's shape in the roughed out parts, I prefer to sculpt with a rasp. While making long sweeps you will be establishing a flat. When I round over a surface with a rasp or the grinder, I make a series of contiguous flats and then join them with flats until they form a radius that pleases me. Start with the big rasps, using sweeping, big muscle strokes. Work on it until it smiles at you!

Remember the best tools in your kit are patience, persistence and a positive attitude!

the sculptor's tools

I have listed these tools in descending order based on their use for shaping and sculpting large to small surfaces. I provide some general and specific recommendations for each tool type.

1 Large area tools *(L= Large)* shape or sculpt large surfaces. Most of these tools will rough shape the surfaces to various degrees. An example would be shaping the sweep of the arms.

2 Small area tools *(S = Small)* can rough shape and refine a surface ready to finish with some sanding.

3 Some tools can work large and small areas effectively *(B = Both)*. Many large tools can work small but is harder to be effective with a small tool on a large surface.

Band Saw (L)
It provides the general profile of the entire chair and is essential to this work. You will need a minimum of a 14" band saw with a riser block to provide more than 7 1/8" under the guides. I use 1/4" (6TPI) or 3/8" (4TPI) hook or skip tooth blades on my saw. For heavier, large radius re-saw cuts a 1/2" blade is sometimes necessary especially for a saw with less than 1 HP.

Angle Grinder (B)
The 4 1/2"grinder (Figures 9.4 & 9.5) is a tool you will use more and more as you gain confidence in your control and know where your chair is in each piece. The grinder can be outfitted with different types of wheels (chain saw, carbide) and/or sandpaper to shape and sculpt seat contours and all other large areas.

figure 9.4

figure 9.5

It is also possible to contour small areas like the seat to front leg joint radius with practice.

My favorite is the RAS 115 by Festool (Figure 9.5) with a 22E Dust Extractor. It is shown in the video with 24 grit Saphir sandpaper and a hard packing pad. The reasons I prefer this combo is it has great control and outstanding fine dust extraction. Before I began using the Festool I used a grinder with a donut shaped carbide wheel.

figure 9.6

It cuts great but it is messy and bad for your lungs. With both of these I use a dust mask or its equivalent.

Rasps (B)
Rasps for shaping large surfaces are longer, wider and coarser. They can be used to shape the entire chair with the exception of the seat to leg joint radii.

My favorites are Auriou rasps (Figure 9.6). The number system I describe relates to them. The lower number the coarser the cut. The higher number makes a finer the cut. The Auriou rasps are hand-stitched meaning their teeth are set by hand making the tooth arrangement void of a pattern.

The result is that they leave a much smoother cut that is not furrowed or torn-out if the rasp is used correctly. They also have teeth right up to and along the edge, allowing the sculptor to get into corners and crevices. They are a much harder cut on your wallet in that they average $100+ for each rasp. A set of three rasps will take care of a great many of your needs.

The first Auriou rasps I grab are the Albi Combination *(L)* flat #5 on one side #9 on the other and a big #9 or#10 Cabinetmakers Rasp *(B)* that is curved on one side and flat on the other and comes to a point. Use big muscles and make long sweeps focusing on holding the rasp at 45 degrees to the length of the piece of wood while pushing the rasp along the stock's length. Do not saw with the rasp. When the cut is cleanest you have found its best working angle. Look at the rasp's teeth and push the teeth in that direction.

For detail I like the #13 Modeler's Rasp *(S)*. It leaves a very clean surface and provides great definition. Use this for final definition of the surfaces, lines and radii around the seat to leg and arm joints.

There are other choices. Sam Maloof used Nicholson's Patternmaker's Rasps *(B)*. They are the best of those not hand stitched. The #49 might be the only rasp you need.

Microplanes *(S)* are used like rasps and are great tools for sculpting. I like the blades you can place in handles. Some of the blades have a radius that is very useful because their shape is the one you would like to carve into a particular surface. For example in the video I use a 3" Microplane in a handle to carve a tight radius in the back leg to backrest joint. You can actually lay them on their side and cut into one surface without cutting an opposing one. Another plus is that you can push or pull in spite of grain orientation, whichever works best.

Flex-Shaft Grinders (S)

There are several different types of die grinders. Flexible shaft (Figure 9.7), pneumatic and self-contained electric models are all capable of shaping and carving the small areas. The characteristics I look for are 1/3HP power, acceptance of 1/4"diameter shank cutters, durability and ease in setting the optimal rpm for the material and the cutter.

My favorite for fairing in the leg to seat, arm to leg joints and everything in between is the Foredom Industrial THX 440. It features a 1/3HP permanent magnet, all ball bearing non-reversible motor for all the power you will need to move a lot of stock quickly and with great control. The 39" flexible shaft is longer and heavier which means you can go where you want to go. The cast iron SXR foot-operated speed control is great but I purchased the bench-top rheostat so I could operate at a steady speed. The 44HT hand-piece is heavy duty and takes 1/8" & 1/4" collets. Ninety-five percent of the time I'm using burrs with 1/4" shafts.

Cutter Burrs

Try an assortment of carbide cutters. The way I select them depends on the shape of the burr as related to the surfaces I want to carve and the necessary coarseness required. My desire is to use the least coarse that will do the job the quickest with the most control.

The following is a list of 1/4" shank carbide burrsthat will take care of most of your requirements:

figure 9.7

1 Flame 3/8"/ Medium or Fine
2 Ball-Nose 3/4" X 1 1/4"/Coarse or Extra-Coarse
3 Smooth-End Cylinder 3/4" X 1 1/4"/ Medium or Coarse
4 Sphere (Figure 9.7) 5/8" and 1/2" Diameters/ Medium and Fine

Scrapers (B)

The hand scraper is just a piece of steel with a burr raised on the edge but it does a marvelous job of removing rasp and other tool marks. The scraper is my tool of choice for cleaning up and final shaping of a surface. It is a must to learn to use one to accomplish fine woodworking projects built from hardwoods.

My recommendation is to purchase thick and thin rectangular scrapers *(B)* along with a set with various sizes and radii *(S)*. A gooseneck scraper may substitute for the set as it offers many varied radii. I prefer a thin flexible scraper for details.

reconciliation of one side of the chair to the other

The hardest part of sculpting a chair is what I call reconciliation. That is balancing the right arm with the left arm or making them mirror images. The best tool I have for reconciliation is sight. If it doesn't look right it probably is not right. Sometimes differences in grain between the two parts can be misleading. That is when I get out the old multi-fingered copiers, calipers, and the kitchen sink to verify various radii, heights, widths and distances between points. An example would be the distance of the front tips of each the arms from a point on the pommel. Do this until it looks right.

workbook activity 1
the front view

Directions: Make some copies of this page for activity use only. Use a contrasting gel pen and draw the contour lines and hard lines on the front view picture.

workbook activity 2
the side view

Directions: Make some copies of this page for activity use only. Use a contrasting gel pen and draw the contour lines and hard lines on the side view picture.

A2

workbook activity 3
the back view

Directions: Make some copies of this page for activity use only. Use a contrasting gel pen and draw the contour lines and hard lines on the back view picture.

appendix

Schedule and Check List for Assembling the Low Back Dining Chair with Glue

Leg up the seat with screws and glue when:
____ Joinery is complete
____ Legs rough shaped
____ Seat sides, back and front shaped
____ Seat is shaped and sanded

Assemble the arm to leg joints with glue and screws when:
____ Arm joint fits the front leg and back leg flush
____ Arm is shaped except for fairing the leg joints
____ Back leg to seat joints have been faired and sanded

Assemble, screw and glue the backrest to the back legs when:
____ Backrest is shaped and fits between the back legs snuggly with screws in place
____ Shaping and sanding is complete on insides of back leg and seat
____ Bottom profile of the headrest is rough shaped and ready to be faired into the back leg

GLUE RECCOMENDATIONS

One of the top ten questions I hear is concerning glue choices. Everybody has their favorite. Some people have cited tests from Fine Woodworking and others. There are many types of glue that will do a great job and I haven't tried them all.
These are my recommendations for the following glue ups:
Titebond Extended Open Time - Seat, Seat to Leg Joints, Arm to Legs, Headrest to Back leg, Rocker Laminations (I tint the laminate glue with a brown water dye so the glue joint won't show through the sculpted laminations)
Franklin Liquid Hide Glue -Spindles to Seat and to Headrest
West System 3 Epoxy - Attaching Rockers to Legs with Dowels

SANDING

I dislike sanding, and I know you do too! I wear a breathing apparatus that makes me look like a scuba diver, not one at peace with the joys of working wood. My best results come from a mixture of hand sanding and power sanding. The choice is made according to the needs and shape of the surface. After shaping, I sand all surfaces with the highest effective grit that will remove tool marks and abrasions and leave its own scratch pattern after sanding completely. Sometimes it may be as low as 60 grit, but for most of the chair is usually 100 grit. Starting at that point, I go through the complete schedule of 100, 120, 150, 180, 220, 320 and finally 400. Before finishing I will vigorously rub the entire chair with a red, gray and finish with a white 3M pad. This leaves the surface almost burnished at 1000 grit.

FINISH

Make Your Own
The traditional finish is a 3 - 4 coat of 1/3 Tung oil, 1/3 boiled linseed oil and 1/3 satin varnish applied with a rag. It is followed by a mixture of the same oils above leaving out the varnish and instead adding a grated handful of beeswax. This is heated slowly in a double boiler or crock pot until the wax melts. After cooling it will be a heavy cream.

Waterlox and Wax
I have used Waterlox instead of the three-part oil mixture listed above. I like the way it builds. The way I prepare the oil and wax mixture above is in a low temperature crock-pot in an area without other flammable materials nearby. At about 140 degrees the wax will finally melt. When it cools it is ready to start rubbing.

Masterpiece Oil and Wax Finish
I helped develop this finish to make it easier to obtain a beautiful oil and wax finish. Safely heating the beeswax and oil to the correct temperature is a roadblock for many woodworkers. Masterpiece is a 3 part system that begins with an oil basecoat, followed by an oil and wax midcoat that will build and fill up the wood's pores and finally a hard wax topcoat that will provide great protection and controllable luster.

The oils can be applied with a rag or paper towel. After 24 hours rub them out with a gray Scotchbrite pad. The oil and wax mixtures should be applied with your hand and rubbed until friction heats your hand and the finish. Then apply the finish wax if you use Masterpiece in thin coats, buffing each vigorously.

TOOL LIST

I have provided a partial tool list. A more complete list can be found at my website. Work-a-rounds and substitutions for most tools on the list are available. Contact me at rocknchairman@gmail.com or visit www.charlesbrockchairmaker.com.

Preparing Stock:	Bandsaw-14" or larger w/riser, 8" jointer, 10" Table Saw, Planer
Producing Parts from Template:	Band Saw, Router Table, 2" Spiral Trim Bit
Coopering the Seat:	Festool Domino or Freud Dowel Joiner or biscuit joiner, Band Saw, Grinder w/ 4" carbide Kutzall (Blue Donut Shaped), Sander w/ 24 Grit Sandpaper
Seat to Leg Joinery:	Router, Router Table w/ Fence, Whiteside Router Bits (Bits must have matching radii!) Rabbet bit #1922 (1 ½" diameter) ¾" Round-over Bit #2010, Crosscut Sled, Small Router Plane
Layout/ Marking:	Colored Pencils, White-Red-Black, No.2 Pencils, Sharpies, Chalk, Marking Knife, Dividers, Tape Measure, Rule, Squares, Protractor, Bevel Boss, Sliding Bevel
Front Legs:	Table Saw, Miller Dowel Bit 1X or 1XJ, 1/2" Brad Point Bit, Electric Drill, Band Saw
Shaping Tools:	Die Grinder w/ Various Burrs, Various Burrs and Rasps, Router w/ ¾" and 1 ¼" Round-over Bits, Microplanes - All Sizes & Shapes, Woodworker's Vise Mounted On Workbench
Sanding:	Sandpaper 60-400 Grit for Hand Sanding, 3M Pads: Maroon, Gray, White
Miscellaneous:	Veritas Tenon Cutters: (Round Blade Model) 3/8" & 1/2", Block Plane, Dowel-It

Seat Clamping Jig:
Cut List: 1@ 3/4" X 22" X 28" Hardwood Plywood
           2@ 3/4" X 3" X 22" Hardwood Plywood
Directions: Glue and screw the 3 X 22" Strips to the larger piece and drill a 3/4-inch through hole to accept the Veritas Wonder Pups in the center of each strip.

Depth Gauge:
Cut List: 1@ 3/4 X 1" X 24" Harwood or Plywood
          1 or more 4" lengths of 1/4" or 3/8" dowel - chamfered on one end
Directions: Find the center of the 24" stock and drill several holes 1" apart on one side of the centerline to span one half of the seat bowl width. Insert the dowel(s). Resting the strip across the width of the seat, plunge the dowel or dowels down like fingers until they bottom out. Flip the stick around to compare the depth on the other side.

Cut List and Bill of Materials
   Seat: 5@ 8/4 X 4 1/4" X 22"
   Front Legs: 2@ 8/4 X 2 13/16" X 21"
   Back Legs: 2@ 8/4 X 6 1/2" 30 1/8"
   Arms: 2@ 8/4 X 3/4" X 22"
   Backrest: 1@ 8/4 X 7 1/8" X 14 1/2"
   Spax Screws: 14 @ #10 X 3" & 2 @ #10 X 2 1/2"
   Ebony Plugs: 16
   Oak Dowel: 1@ 1/2" X Market Length
   Festool Dominos: 12@ 8 X 40mm

PLUGS

I make my plugs from ½" thick X ½" wide sticks of ebony. One 12 inch stick will provide enough for a chair. I make a tapered plug for each hole using the same Veritas 3/8" tenon maker that I use on the headrest end of the spindle. Place the stick in a vise and use it like a pencil sharpener. Test it in the hole and mark it for cutting off. Place it back in the vise cut it off the stick leaving an extra 1/4 ". Add glue and tap it in until it stops. Cut and sand it flush when it dries. A scraper comes in handy for final surfacing.

sam maloof
Who Inspired Us All

There would not be a "Build a Sculptured Low Back Chair with Charles Brock" without Sam Maloof. I recently taught a woodworking class on the subject of the rocker in a room Maloof himself taught in. There were two huge pictures of him hanging on the walls and I felt like he was with me guiding me along.

I spent a weekend with him in Atlanta several years ago at a workshop. Sam was a humble genius at work even though there were problems with the equipment. He never stopped or complained. He worked and taught wonderfully as if everything was perfect.

Sam was an icon in so many ways. He made a living doing what he wanted to do. Instead of selling his designs to be manufactured or mass-produced, he built them one at a time. He rose well beyond the title he loved- "woodworker." Sam Maloof has become the most inspiring furniture maker and designer of the late 20th century.

Sam brought his gifted visions to functional forms that serve as inspirations for us all.